A DISH
FOR A WISH

BROUGHT TO YOU BY
RAYS OF SUNSHINE
CHILDREN'S CHARITY

First published 2013 in Great Britain
by Rays of Sunshine Children's Charity
Registered Charity No. 1102529

©2013 Rays of Sunshine Children's Charity

Rays of Sunshine Children's Charity
No. 1 Olympic Way
Wembley
Middlesex HA9 0NP
Telephone 020 8782 1171
Fax 020 8782 1173
raysofsunshine.org.uk
info@raysofsunshine.org.uk

All rights reserved. No part of this publication may be reproduced in any form or by any electronic means (including photocopying, recording, or information storage and retrieval) without permission in writing from the publisher.

A CIP record of this book is available at the British Library.

ISBN 978-0-9572474-1-3

Project concept by Laura Barnett
Edited by Laura Barnett,
Rays of Sunshine Children's Charity

Designed by Em-Project Limited
Telephone 01892 614 346
mike@em-project.com
em-project.com

Printed by L&S Printing
ls-printing.com

Rays of Sunshine would like to thank:
Laura Barnett for her passion in turning this cook book into a tasty reality; our celebrity supporters who have contributed to this book; Mike Turner for helping to make this book possible.

Rays of Sunshine Children's Charity grants wishes for seriously ill children in the UK aged 3-18.

Every day of the year the charity gives brave and deserving young people the chance to put their illness on hold and enjoy a magical moment.

Rays of Sunshine
Granting Magical Wishes Everyday

FULL ENGLISH
from Louis Smith
40

3

Recipe courtesy of The Breakfast Club

Welcome to Rays of Sunshine's second celebrity cookbook, **A Dish for a Wish, Morning Sunshine.** All the profits from this book will help our charity to continue to brighten up the lives of seriously ill children.

There are 40,000 children in the UK living with a serious or life limiting illness. Our mission is to give these young people and their families the chance to put their illness aside and create a memory that will last forever.

We always say that wishes are as unique as the children themselves and I can't think of a better example of this than our 3,000th wish for 8-year-old Lauren to meet a 'real life' mermaid. Seeing Lauren's face when she spotted a mermaid swimming near the shores of Loch Lomond, typified the joy and excitement we bring to brave children's lives every day.

We are so grateful to our famous supporters for giving up their time to help make wishes come true and for sharing their favourite breakfast and brunch recipes with us. We hope that this book will help turn every breakfast into a special occasion.

If you'd like to buy further copies for friends or find out how you can donate or get more involved with the charity please visit the Rays of Sunshine website **www.raysofsunshine.org.uk**

Jane Sharpe
Chief Executive
Rays of Sunshine Children's Charity

5

6

Introduction

Leading chef Lorraine Pascale, owns her own successful Covent Garden bakery, Ella's Bakehouse. Her two primetime cookery series on BBC2 attracted millions of viewers and her three cookery books were all bestsellers. Lorraine's new book 'A Lighter Way to Bake' is out now.

I am proud to be an ambassador for Rays of Sunshine. Over the last couple of years I have had the pleasure of meeting and cooking with some truly wonderful children, and they have all really impressed me with their amazing knowledge of cooking. These young people have all shown an incredible strength of character and I only hope they are able to grow up and fulfil their ambitions to become chefs.

This fabulous book contains a whole host of scrumptious recipes for breakfast and brunch which have been lovingly donated to Rays of Sunshine to help make more wishes come true. Whether your favourite breakfast is a healthy granola or an indulgent pancake you can find the recipe here. Most of all I hope you start your day with a smile.

Lorraine Pascale
Ambassador

10/SOMETHING SIMPLE
12/Nell McAndrew
My perfect porridge
14/Jamie Oliver
Super quick granola
18/Gwyneth Paltrow
Blythe's blueberry muffins

20/JLS
Smoothie
24/Kate Moss
French toast with crispy bacon and maple syrup
26/Boris Johnson
Cheese on toast
28/Pixie Lott
Granola

30/SOMETHING WITH EGGS
32/Gordon Ramsay
Pan fried egg with aubergine caponata and anchovy dressing
36/Kelly Brook
Spanish omelette

38/Gary Rhodes
Scrambled egg mushroom muffins
40/Louis Smith
Full English (Full Monty)
42/Giraffe
Huevos rancheros ranch style eggs tostada

44/Gino D'Acampo
Mediterranean eggs
48/Vivek Singh
Ham and egg dosa
52/England Footballers Foundation (EFF)
Scrambled eggs with ham and cheese
56/Olly Murs
Ham and mushroom omelette

8

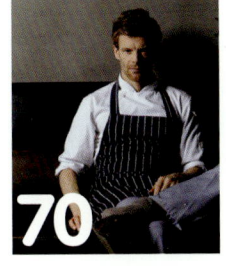

58/SOMETHING SWEETER
60/Tana Ramsay
Ricotta pancakes with honeycomb butter
64/Lisa Snowdon
Pancakes made with buckwheat and served with blueberries
65/Claudia Winkleman
Pancakes with maple syrup

66/Myleene Klass
Pancakes with bacon, maple syrup and berries
67/Emma Bunton
Pancakes with maple syrup and fruit
68/Rochelle Wiseman
Blueberry pancakes
70/Tom Aikens
Blueberry and buttermilk pancakes

74/SOMETHING DIFFERENT
76/One Direction
Burrito
78/James Martin
Baked New York raspberry cheesecake
82/Kimberley Walsh
Heaven waffles

84/Bill Granger
Leek and spinach cake
88/Lorraine Pascale
Aussie sweetcorn breakfast fritters with avocado and rocket salad and sweet chilli jam
92/Leona Lewis
Tofu scramble
94/Pippa Middleton
Full English frittata

96/Amanda Lamb
Vanilla cheesecake
100/THANK YOU
102/Wishes
Our wish children

9

"RAYS OF SUNSHINE PUTS SMILES ON THE FACES OF SERIOUSLY ILL CHILDREN EVERY DAY. AS A MUM I KNOW HOW IMPORTANT THIS IS AND I AM THRILLED TO SUPPORT THEM DURING THEIR 10TH BIRTHDAY YEAR."

Nell McAndrew

SOMETHING SIMPLE

"MY FAVOURITE BREAKFAST IS EASY TO PREPARE IN A RUSH AND WILL PROVIDE YOU WITH LASTING ENERGY."

12

MY PERFECT PORRIDGE ENERGY IN A BOWL MADE WITH HALF SOYA MILK/HALF WATER TOPPED WITH SPRINKLING OF LINUSPROUT, BLUEBERRIES AND BANANA

from Nell McAndrew
Serves 1

Ingredients
- 50g porridge oats
- 175ml soya milk
- 175ml water
- Sprinkling of linusprout, sprouted flaxseed powder
- 1 medium banana
- Handful of blueberries

Method
- Put the oats in a saucepan, pour in the soya milk gradually add the water and add a tiny pinch of salt. Bring to the boil and simmer for 4-5 minutes, stirring from time to time and watching carefully that it doesn't stick to the bottom of the pan.
- Leave to stand for 2 minutes.
- Stir in the bananas and add the blueberries on top.

"GRANOLA IS THE PERFECT PORTABLE BREAKFAST. THIS WILL GIVE YOU A BIG BATCH SO, AS SOON AS IT'S COOL, TIP IT INTO A TUB OR LARGE JAM JAR, THEN TAKE IT TO WORK WITH A POT OF YOGURT AND A COUPLE OF PUNNETS OF BERRIES AND YOU'RE SORTED FOR A GOOD FEW DAYS."

Jamie Oliver
SUPER QUICK GRANOLA

15

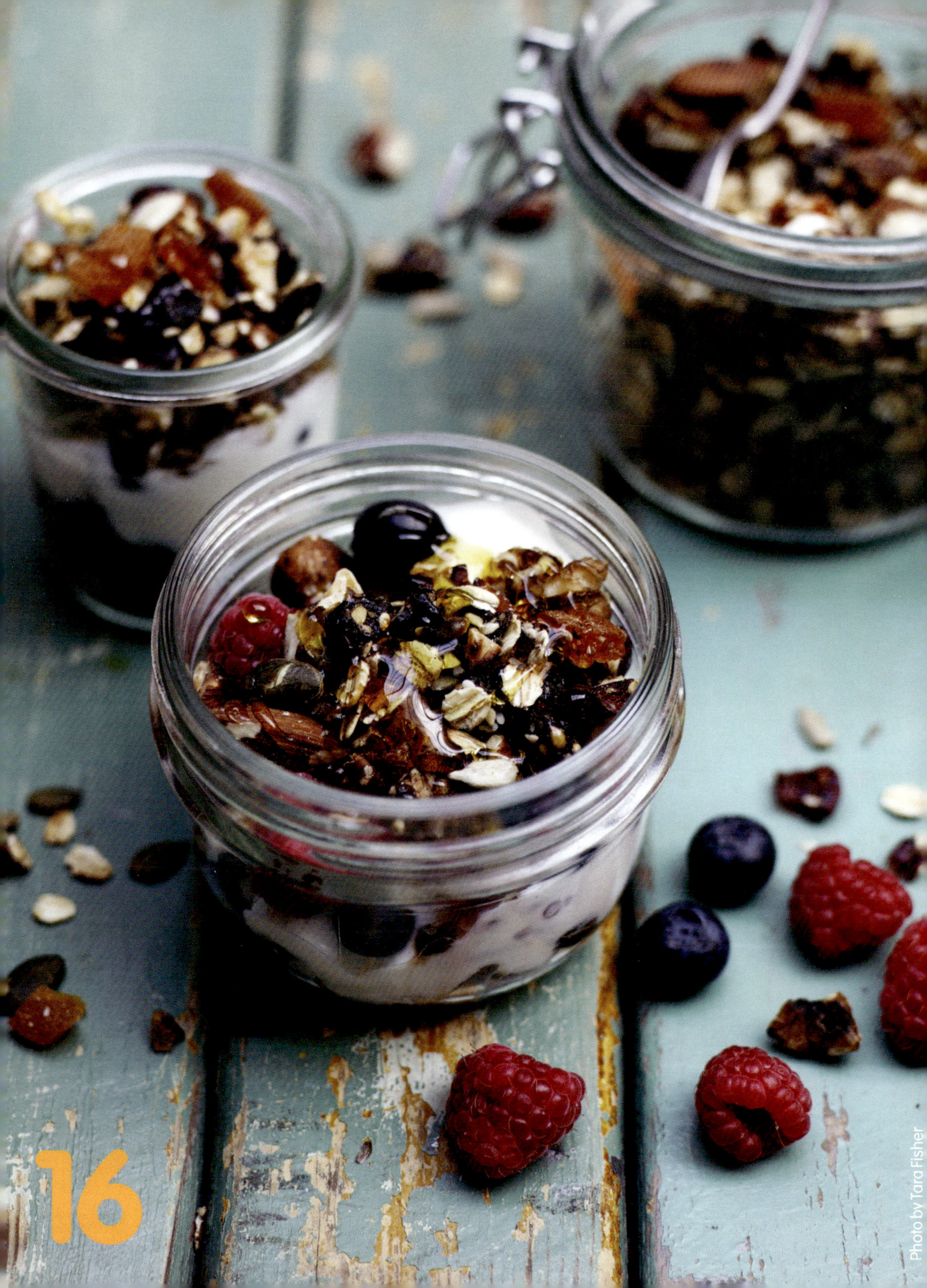
Photo by Tara Fisher

SUPER QUICK GRANOLA
from Jamie Oliver
Makes 10 portions

Ingredients
- 130g mixed nuts, such as walnuts and pecans, roughly chopped
- 50g mixed seeds, such as sunflower and pumpkin
- 130g dried fruit, such as apricots, sour cherries and cranberries, roughly chopped
- 50g rolled oats
- 2 tbsp runny honey
- Low-fat natural yoghurt, to serve
- Fresh seasonal berries, to serve

Method
- Add the nuts, seeds, dried fruit and oats to a large frying pan on a high heat and toast for 5-10 minutes or until golden and smelling fantastic. Make sure you toss the pan often to stop it from catching.
- Remove from the heat, drizzle with the honey and jiggle the pan to coat, then leave to cool. Meanwhile, mash up some fresh berries and swirl them through natural yoghurt.
- Layer up the granola in little pots with the fruity yoghurt. Sprinkle over more fresh berries or other seasonal fruit and serve.

BLYTHE'S BLUEBERRY MUFFINS
from Gwyneth Paltrow
Serves 12

Ingredients
- 120g unsalted butter, melted and cooled slightly
- 2 eggs (preferably organic)
- 250ml whole milk
- 250g sunbleached all-purpose flour
- 150g plus 1 tsp sugar, divided
- 2 tsp baking powder
- ½ tsp salt
- 450g fresh blueberries

Method
- Heat oven to 190°C.
- Line a 12-cup muffin pan with paper liners.
- Whisk butter, eggs and milk in a bowl.
- Combine flour, 150g sugar, baking powder and salt in another bowl.
- Stir wet ingredients into dry ingredients; fold in blueberries.
- Divide batter evenly among muffin cups; sprinkle with remaining 1 tsp sugar.
- Bake until muffins are golden brown and a knife comes out clean, 25-30 minutes.
- Serve warm.

From **My Father's Daughter: Delicious, Easy Recipes Celebrating Family & Togetherness** by Gwyneth Paltrow

"WHEN I WAS PREGNANT, I ASKED MY MOTHER TO MAKE THESE FOR ME ALL THE TIME. THEY'RE JUST THE RIGHT BALANCE OF TART AND SWEET."

19

"WE LOVE BEING PART OF THE RAYS OF SUNSHINE FAMILY. WE HAVE BEEN PROUD TO WATCH THE

20

CHARITY GROW OVER THE LAST FIVE YEARS AND ARE ALL COMMITTED TO CONTINUE TO HELP OUT WHENEVER WE CAN."

JLS

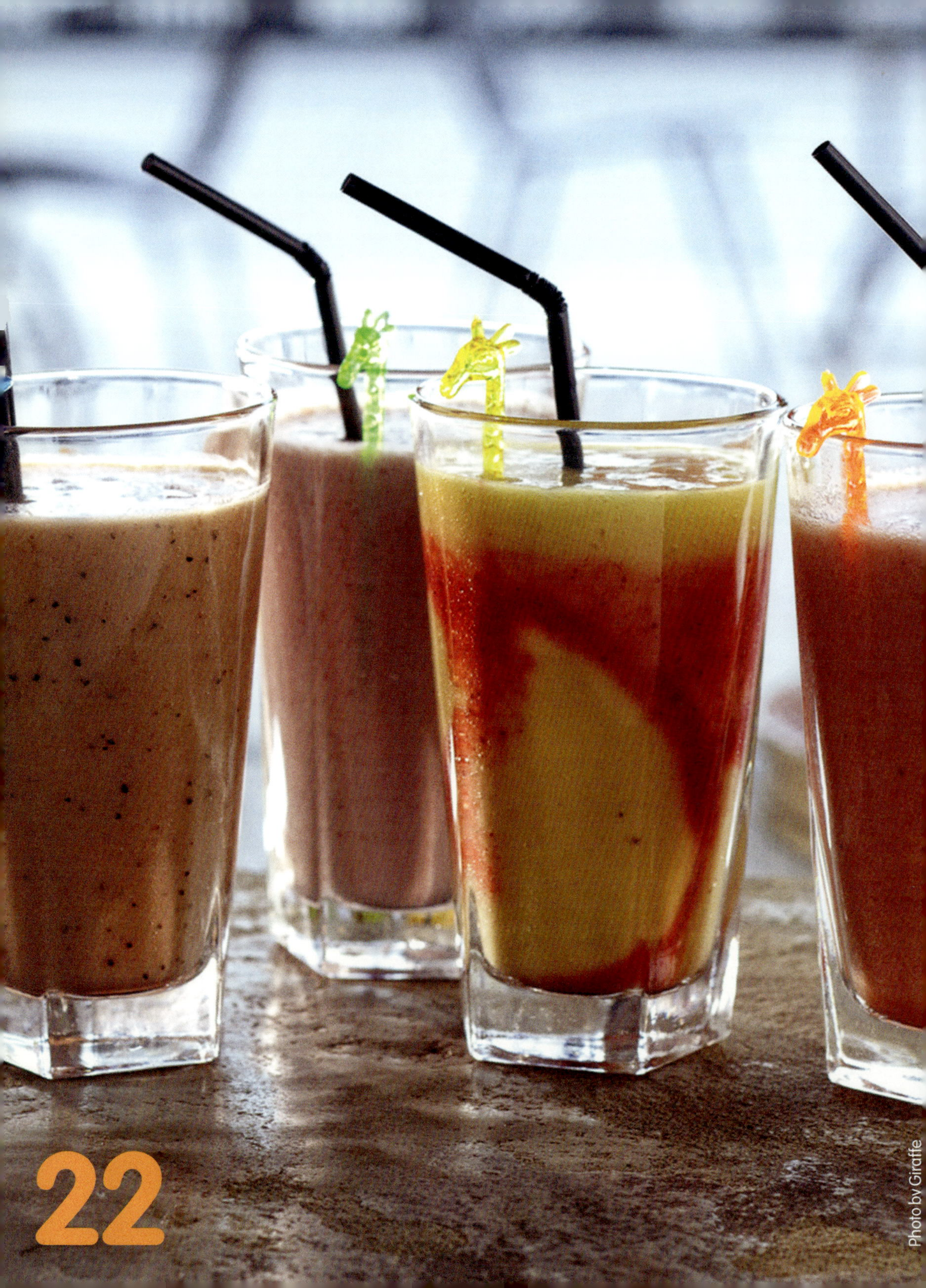

Photo by Giraffe

— **Sunrise smoothie**
from JLS
Serves 1

— **"IN A BLENDER COMBINE A SMALL HANDFUL OF CRUSHED ICE, HALF A FRESH BANANA, 25ML OF STRAWBERRY PUREE OR A HANDFUL OF FRESH STRAWBERRIES AND 125ML OF FRESH ORANGE JUICE. BLEND UNTIL SMOOTH THEN POUR INTO A GLASS AND ENJOY!"**

FRENCH TOAST WITH CRISPY BACON AND MAPLE SYRUP
from Kate Moss
Serves 4

Ingredients
- 1 tbsp vegetable oil
- 80g butter
- 3 tbsp milk
- 3 eggs
- 2 tbsp caster sugar
- 8 thick slices white bread
- 8 slices maple back cured bacon
- Maple syrup

Method
- Heat a frying pan over a moderate heat and add the olive oil. Fry the bacon on both sides until crispy. Remove and drain on kitchen paper. Add the butter to the pan and remove from the heat.
- Combine the milk, eggs and sugar, and whisk.
- Return the pan to the heat. Dip the bread in the egg mixture and fry until golden brown. Keep warm until you use up all the bread.
- Serve the fried bread with the crispy bacon and a generous drizzle of maple syrup.

25

Photo by Pietro Birindelli

26

CHEESE ON TOAST
from Boris Johnson
Serves as many as you like

Ingredients
- Cheese, preferably cheddar
- Brown bread
- Butter and/or chutney

Method
- Cut a large amount of cheese, preferably cheddar, into slabs.
- Lightly toast some brown bread.
- Spread toast with butter and chutney.
- Cover toast with slabs of cheese.
- Grill until it gets all nice and scabby.

—GRANOLA
from Pixie Lott
Serves 4

—Ingredients
- 450g rolled oats
- 120g sunflower seeds
- 100g coconut flakes
- 120g golden syrup
- 4 tbsp runny honey
- 100g soft light brown sugar
- 250g whole almonds
- 1 tsp salt
- 2 tbsp sunflower oil

Toppings
- 10 strawberries, cut in half
- 100g blueberries
- 300g Greek style yoghurt
- Squeeze of runny honey

—Method
- Mix all the ingredients together in a mixing bowl.
- Spread the mixture onto two baking trays and bake in a fan oven at 170°C.
- Stir the ingredients after around 20 minutes and put back in the oven for another 20 minutes or so, until it is evenly toasted.
- This can be stored in an airtight container.

To assemble
- Mix the berries together.
- Best served in 4 tumbler glasses.
- Place a spoonful of granola at the bottom of each glass.
- Add a spoonful of berries, followed by a spoonful of yoghurt. Add a squeeze of honey followed by a second spoonful of granola.

29

"I AM ABSOLUTELY HONOURED TO BE AN AMBASSADOR FOR RAYS OF SUNSHINE, IT'S A GREAT CHARITY. IT'S SO LOVELY TO MEET SO MANY AMAZING CHILDREN AND HELP THE CHARITY TO SPREAD MORE BEAUTIFUL SMILES".

Pixie Lott

SOMETHING WITH EGGS

31

"I HAVE BEEN FORTUNATE ENOUGH TO MEET SOME FANTASTIC CHILDREN THROUGH RAYS OF SUNSHINE THIS YEAR. THESE CHILDREN ARE SO INSPIRING AND I REALLY HOPE THAT THEY GROW UP TO FULFIL THEIR AMBITIONS AND LIVE THEIR DREAMS."

Gordon Ramsay

33

34

PAN FRIED EGG WITH AUBERGINE CAPONATA AND ANCHOVY DRESSING
from Gordon Ramsay
Serves 1

Ingredients
For the caponata
- 1 aubergine
- 2 shallots
- ½ bunch basil
- 4 tomato
- 1 sprig thyme

For the anchovy dressing
- 150g extra virgin olive oil
- 20g pine nuts
- ½ lemon zest
- 15g lemon juice
- 1 tbsp parsley
- 10g parmesan
- 15g anchovy
- 30g confit shallots
- 60g black olives

For the egg and baguette
- 1 Burford Brown egg
- 1 small baguette

Method
To cook the caponata
- Place seasoned aubergine, shallot, garlic and tomatoes in a pan and roast in oven with extra virgin olive oil until fully cooked.
- Combine the anchovy dressing.
- Fry one Burford Brown egg. Thinly slice baguette and toast with olive oil and thyme.
- To plate, place the warmed caponata in the middle of the plate. Top with fried egg. Finish with anchovy dressing and crustini.
- Serve.

SPANISH OMELETTE
from Kelly Brook
Serves 2

Ingredients
- 500g potatoes
- 1 onion
- 150ml olive oil
- 3 tbsp chopped flatleaf parsley
- 6 eggs

Method
- Peel and slice the potatoes. Rinse, drain and dry.
- Chop the onion.
- Heat the oil in a large frying pan, add the potatoes and onion and sauté gently, partially covered, until the potatoes are softened – stir occasionally.
- Strain the potatoes and onions through a colander into a large bowl (save the strained liquid).
- Beat the eggs one by one, then stir into the potatoes with the parsley and plenty of salt and pepper. Heat a little of the strained oil in a smaller pan. Tip everything into the pan and cook on a moderate heat.
- When almost set, turn the omelette over by holding a plate on the pan and cook for a few minutes on the other side. Turn the omelette once more on each side. Slide onto a plate. Allow to cool slightly before serving.

37

38

SCRAMBLED EGG MUSHROOM MUFFINS
from Gary Rhodes
Serves 2-4

Ingredients
- 2 muffins, halved
- 15g butter, plus extra for spreading and scrambling
- 100g mushrooms, sliced or quartered
- 6 eggs
- Salt and pepper
- 1 heaped tsp chopped chives
- Parmesan cheese, for grating

Method
- Preheat the grill. Brush each muffin half with butter and toast under the grill until golden.
- Melt the butter in a frying pan and, once foaming, add the mushrooms and fry over a medium to hot heat for 1 or 2 minutes until softened.
- Spoon on top of the muffins.
- Meanwhile, beat the eggs to combine the yolks with the whites. Melt a large knob of butter in a saucepan or frying pan and, once bubbling but before it browns, pour in the eggs, seasoning them with salt and pepper.
- Turn and stir the eggs fairly vigorously with a wooden spoon, covering every corner of the pan.
- Top the muffins with the scrambled eggs, sprinkle over the chives and grate parmesan cheese on top of each one.

FULL ENGLISH (FULL MONTY)
from Louis Smith
Serves 2

Ingredients
- 4 large free range eggs
- 2 good quality pork sausages
- 4 rashers of un-smoked, dry cured back bacon
- 2 slices of black pudding
- 2 slices of multigrain toast
- 1 tin of baked beans
- 1 beef tomato, cut in half
- 2 portobello mushroom
- Garlic clove, butter, olive oil, salt and pepper
- 1 or 2 large maris piper potatoes
- 1 medium white onion
- Fresh oregano
- Fresh curly parsley
- Olive oil
- Salt and pepper

Recipe courtesy of
The Breakfast Club

Method
- Wash potatoes to remove any dirt. Cut into large chunks. Add to cold salted water and bring to the boil. Allow to boil for approximately 5 minutes until slightly softened. Drain.
- To make the seasoning for the potatoes finely chop a handful of oregano and parsley. Place in a bowl and add a good pinch of sea salt and freshly ground black pepper. Add 25ml of olive oil and mix thoroughly .
- Pour the dressing into a heated frying pan and add the potato chunks and the onion to the pan, fry until the potatoes are cooked through and golden brown. Store in an oven proof dish in a warm oven until ready to serve.
- Heat the grill, place two plates on the bottom of the oven to warm through. Put the sausages on a tray to cook for around 10-15 minutes, add the bacon rashers and cook to your preference, the longer the crispier.
- Put the baked beans in a saucepan and warm gently for 2-3 minutes, stirring occasionally. Pop the multigrain bread into the toaster. When done butter and put a slice on each plate.
- Finely chop a clove of garlic and add to a hot frying pan with a drizzle of olive oil. Add the mushrooms and beef tomato halves and cook over a low heat so as to not burn the garlic, season with sea salt and pepper. A touch of fresh basil works really well too. When cooked, transfer to a plate and keep warm on the bottom shelf of the grill oven. Brush away the garlic from the pan and add another drizzle of olive oil .Crack the eggs into the pan, cook and season.
- Portion all the ingredients onto your warmed plates and tuck in!

41

PUTTING BREAKFAST ON AN OPEN TORTILLA IS JUST ONE OF THOSE IDEAS THAT MAKES SUCH PERFECT SENSE. IF YOU ARE IN A HURRY, OR JUST LIKE TO EAT WITH YOUR FINGERS, YOU CAN ROLL IT UP. OR SETTLE DOWN WITH A KNIFE AND FORK. IT'S ALL SUMMER SUNSHINE, BRIGHT COLOURS AND PACKED FULL OF FLAVOUR. A WAKE-UP CALL TO BE RECOMMENDED!

HUEVOS RANCHEROS
RANCH STYLE EGGS TOSTADA
from Giraffe
Serves 4

Ingredients
- 1 tin of black beans
- 100g tinned sweetcorn, rinsed and drained
- 4 flour tortillas
- 20 pieces thinly sliced chorizo
- 2 cups mixed cheddar and mozzarella cheese, grated
- 2 tbsp olive oil
- 8 eggs
- A few sprigs fresh coriander

For the avocado tomato salsa
- 1 avocado, diced
- 1 beef tomato, de-seeded and diced
- 1 small red onion, diced
- 2 tbsp fresh coriander, chopped
- 1 clove garlic, chopped
- 1 spring onion, finely sliced
- 1 red chilli, de-seeded and chopped

For the adobe sauce
- 3 tbsp vegetable oil
- 100g white onions, diced
- 450ml passata or a can of chopped tomatoes
- 25g fresh coriander, chopped
- 25g adobe chillies
- 1 tsp cumin powder
- 1 tsp coriander powder

Method
- Preheat the oven to 190°C.
- Combine in a separate bowl the salsa ingredients and season with salt and pepper. Place to one side.
- Mix the adobe sauce, drained black beans and sweetcorn. Spread a thin layer of this mix onto the tortilla. Place the chorizo slices on the tortilla and sprinkle the cheese on top.
- Place the tortilla on a roasting tray in the oven and cook for 5-6 minutes or until the cheese is bubbling. Keep warm.
- Heat the olive oil in a frying pan and fry the eggs. Take the tortilla from the oven, put two eggs on each one and top with the avocado salsa. Garnish with fresh coriander leaves and serve.

"THIS IS A FANTASTIC WAY TO COOK YOUR EGGS. THE COMBINATION OF THE INGREDIENTS IS JUST UNBELIEVABLE. YOU CAN PREPARE THE SAUCE WELL AHEAD AND WHEN YOU ARE READY, REHEAT IT AND BREAK IN THE EGGS. ENSURE YOU SERVE PLENTY OF BREAD WITH THIS DISH TO SOAK UP THE DELICIOUS SAUCE."

Gino D'Acampo
MEDITTERRANEAN EGGS

45

46

MEDITTERRANEAN EGGS
from Gino D'Acampo
Serves 4

Ingredients
- 3 tbsp olive oil
- 1 medium onion, sliced
- 3 medium courgettes, roughly chopped
- 1 large yellow pepper, roughly chopped
- 400g tinned chopped tomatoes
- 5 fresh basil leaves
- 50g pitted Kalamata olives
- 4 medium eggs
- 70g cheddar cheese, freshly grated
- Salt and pepper

Method
- Heat the olive oil in a large frying pan and fry the onion, courgettes and pepper until soft and browned, stirring occasionally. Season with salt and pepper, add in the tomatoes, basil and olives. Cook uncovered over a medium heat for about 10 minutes or until the water from the tomatoes is well reduced.
- Meanwhile, pre-heat the grill. Make four slight hollows in the tomato mixture and very gently break one egg into each. Sprinkle over the cheese and cook under the grill for about 10 minutes or until the eggs are set as you like them.
- Serve immediately with warm crusty bread.

"THE DOSA IS THE CLASSICAL SOUTHERN INDIAN DISH AND IS EATEN AT ANY TIME DURING THE DAY. TYPICALLY THIS RICE FLOUR PANCAKE IS FILLED WITH SPICY POTATOES BUT CAN LITERALLY HAVE ANYTHING YOU WANT INSIDE. HERE I COMBINE THE BASIC WESTERN HAM AND EGG BREAKFAST WITH THE SOUTHERN INDIAN DOSA PACKAGE."

Vivek Singh,
The Cinnamon Club
HAM AND EGG DOSA

49

50

—HAM AND EGG DOSA
from Vivek Singh,
The Cinnamon Club
Serves 4

—Ingredients
— 200g ready-made dosa mix, available from most Asian stores
— 8 slices of honey roast ham
— 4 eggs
— 3 tbsp oil for cooking
— 200g ready-made dosa mix, available from most Asian stores

—Method
— Stir 300ml water into the dosa mix, then leave aside for 5 minutes for the batter to rise.
— Spread a light amount of oil on a wide flat pan on medium heat. Pour 75ml of the batter in the centre of the pan. Spread quickly with outward circular motion to form a pancake about 20cm in diameter.
— Dot the edges of the pancake with a little oil.
— In the meantime, grill two slices of ham under a grill for 2-3 minutes and break an egg on top of the pancake. While the egg congeals on the pancake, take care not to move it around to prevent the yolk from breaking. Top the egg with the grilled ham and neatly fold from three sides to cover the ham and egg. The pancake should look like a neatly folded triangle now.
— Cook until the egg has settled and the pancake turns golden. Release the pancake from the pan using a spatula.
— Serve with coconut chutney and south Indian lentils also known as sambhar.

"THE ENGLAND FOOTBALLERS FOUNDATION ARE REALLY PROUD TO BE SUPPORTING RAYS OF SUNSHINE THIS YEAR.

"IT'S INSPIRING TO MEET SO MANY AMAZING KIDS AND HELP PUT SMILES ON THEIR FACES."

Joe Hart on behalf of
The England Footballers Foundation

53

"AS FOOTBALLERS, BREAKFAST IS A REALLY IMPORTANT MEAL FOR US. SCRAMBLED EGG WITH CHEESE AND HAM IS ONE OF OUR FAVOURITES."

James Milner

SCRAMBLED EGGS WITH HAM & CHEESE

The England Footballers Foundation
Serves 4

Ingredients
- 8 large eggs
- 2 tsp Worcestershire sauce
- 8 tbsp semi skimmed milk
- Salt and pepper
- 4 slices cooked ham, chopped into bite-size pieces
- 1 cup grated mature cheddar cheese
- Olive oil to grease pan

Method
- Pour a drop of olive oil into a large frying pan and heat over a low heat.
- In a large bowl lightly whisk together the eggs, milk, salt and pepper and Worcestershire sauce.
- Pour the egg mixture into the frying pan and stir continually to avoid sticking.
- Before the egg mixture has completely set stir in the ham and cheese and cook until the ham is hot and the cheese is melted.

—HAM AND MUSHROOM OMELETTE
from Olly Murs
Serves 1

—Ingredients
— 3 large eggs
— 6 white cap mushrooms, washed and dried
— Dash of oil
— Salt and pepper
— Ham hock or sliced ham

—Method
— Chop up ham hock or sliced ham, and slice up the mushrooms.
— Crack the eggs into a bowl and mix together with a fork.
— Pour a dash of oil into a hot pan. Fry the mushrooms off first. Pour the eggs into the pan on the highest heat and leave until it starts bubbling. Tilt the pan so it cooks evenly, then scatter in the ham. Season with salt and black pepper.
— When it starts to set, pull the sides up with a spoon and fold it over. Cook a bit on each half side flipping in between.
— DONE!!! (Eaten within 2 seconds)

57

IT'S AN HONOUR TO BE AN AMBASSADOR FOR RAYS OF SUNSHINE. I HAVE THOROUGHLY ENJOYED MEETING THE AMAZING WISH CHILDREN THEY WORK WITH AND AM LOOKING FORWARD TO MEETING MANY MORE!"

Olly Murs

SOMETHING SWEETER

60

"A DELICIOUS STACK OF PANCAKES IS A DECADENT WAY TO START THE DAY AND GUARANTEED TO PUT A SMILE ON YOUR FACE!"

Tana Ramsay
RICOTTA PANCAKES WITH HONEYCOMB BUTTER

—RICOTTA PANCAKES WITH HONEYCOMB BUTTER
from Tana Ramsay
Serves 2

—Ingredients
For the pancakes
- 112.5g ricotta
- 85ml milk
- 2 eggs separated
- 70g plain flour
- ½ tsp baking powder
- ½ pinch of salt

For the honeycomb
- 195g sugar
- 48g honey
- 75g glucose
- 36ml water
- 10g bicarbonate of soda

—Method
—For the pancakes
Mix the ricotta, milk and egg yolks in a blender. Mix flour, baking powder and salt, slowly add ricotta mixture until just combined. Whisk egg whites until stiff peaks, then fold into the ricotta mixture in two batches. Cook over a low to medium height in gently foaming butter on both sides for 2-3 minutes.

—For the honeycomb
Bring sugar, honey, glucose and water to a boil and bring to a caramel. Add bicarb to the caramel, then transfer to a gastro tray.
- Once honeycomb is cooled, break into small bits.
- In the blender, add one block of butter and 1 cup honeycomb and pulse until fully combined.
- Roll honeycomb butter into logs with clingfilm.

63

HEALTHY LISA SNOWDON LOVES HERS TO BE MADE WITH BUCKWHEAT AND SERVED WITH BLUEBERRIES

CLAUDIA WINKLEMAN ADORES
THE TRADITIONAL DRIZZLE OF
MAPLE SYRUP

65

MYLEENE KLASS PAIRS SWEET AND SAVOURY ON THE SAME PLATE WITH BACON, MAPLE SYRUP AND BERRIES

EMMA BUNTON PREFERS HERS WITH MAPLE SYRUP AND A SIDE ORDER OF FRUIT

67

"WE'VE SPENT SO MUCH TIME IN AMERICA RECENTLY I'VE BECOME REALLY ADDICTED TO THEIR BREAKFASTS! MY FAVOURITE THING ON THE MENU IS ALWAYS BLUEBERRY PANCAKES AND WHEN I'M BACK AT HOME I MAKE THEM FOR MYSELF AND MARVIN. HERE IS MY RECIPE!"

—BLUEBERRY PANCAKES
from Rochelle Wiseman
Serves 2

—Ingredients
— 150g plain flour
— 150g fresh blueberries
— 2 tbsp granulated sugar
— 1 tsp baking powder
— ½ tsp bicarbonate of soda
— Large pinch of salt
— 1 egg
— 240ml milk
— ¼ tsp vanilla extract

—Method
— Whisk together the flour, sugar, bicarbonate of soda, baking powder and salt in a bowl. Add half the milk, the egg and vanilla extract. This should provide you with a great batter.
— Then slowly add the remaining milk and whisk until smooth. Gently add the blueberries and carefully mix them into the batter.
— Lightly oil and heat a non stick frying pan. Drop in 2 tbsp batter per pancake. Cook for 1½-2 minutes until golden underneath and bubbling on top. Flip over and cook for a further 1-2 minutes.
— Serve with lots of maple syrup. Delicious!!

—BLUEBERRY AND BUTTERMILK PANCAKES
from Tom Aikens
Serves 4

71

BLUEBERRY AND BUTTERMILK PANCAKES
from Tom Aikens
Serves 4

Ingredients
- 600g self raising flour
- 125g sugar
- 20g baking powder
- 5g baking soda
- 4g salt
- 600ml buttermilk
- 300ml milk
- 4 eggs
- 115g melted butter
- 10g vanilla essence
- 3g almond essence
- 150g blueberries

Method
- Sift all the dry ingredients together in one bowl, then in another bowl whisk the eggs, milk, buttermilk, vanilla and almond essence together, mix into the dry ingredients and whisk until smooth.
- Add the melted butter next, whisking all the time until mixed in thoroughly.
- Add the blueberries carefully, folding in, then place in a non stick pan and cook until golden in colour.

73

Photo by David Griffin

"WE LOVE BEING AMBASSADORS FOR RAYS OF SUNSHINE. EVEN THOUGH WE HAVE BEEN TOURING THIS YEAR WE HAVE MADE TIME TO MEET WISH CHILDREN, AS GRANTING WISHES IS REALLY IMPORTANT TO US."

One Direction

SOMETHING A LITTLE DIFFERENT

76

BURRITO
from One Direction
Serves 4

Ingredients
- 2 tsp sunflower oil
- ½ small red onion, diced
- 1 red pepper, diced
- 240g tinned black beans, rinsed and drained
- Pinch of chilli flakes
- Salt and freshly ground black pepper
- 4 eggs and 4 egg whites
- 34g cheddar cheese, grated
- 4 tortillas
- 60g sour cream
- 60g salsa
- 1 large tomato, de-seeded and diced
- 1 small avocado, cubed
- Chilli sauce

Method
- Heat the oil in a large frying pan
- Gently cook the onions and peppers until softened – about 8 minutes.
- Add black beans and red pepper – cook until warmed through.
- Season with salt and pepper and transfer to a dish.
- Whisk together the eggs and egg whites and stir in the cheese.
- Lightly grease the pan and heat over a medium heat.
- Reduce heat and add egg mixture, scrambling until cooked through.
- Spread each tortilla with 1 tbsp each sour cream and salsa, then layer with the black bean mixture and scrambled eggs.
- Season, to taste, with hot sauce. Roll up burrito-style and serve.

"NEW YORKERS GET THIS RIGHT, AND THEIR CHEESECAKE SHOULD ONLY BE CHANGED IN TERMS OF THE FLAVOURING. DON'T TAMPER WITH SOMETHING THAT WORKS! IT'S BEST TO SERVE THIS AT ROOM TEMPERATURE, AS I FIND THAT STRAIGHT FROM THE FRIDGE IT'S A BIT LIKE LISTENING TO YOUR BANK MANAGER – HARD WORK AND NOT VERY PLEASANT!"

James Martin
**BAKED NEW YORK
RASPBERRY CHEESECAKE**

79

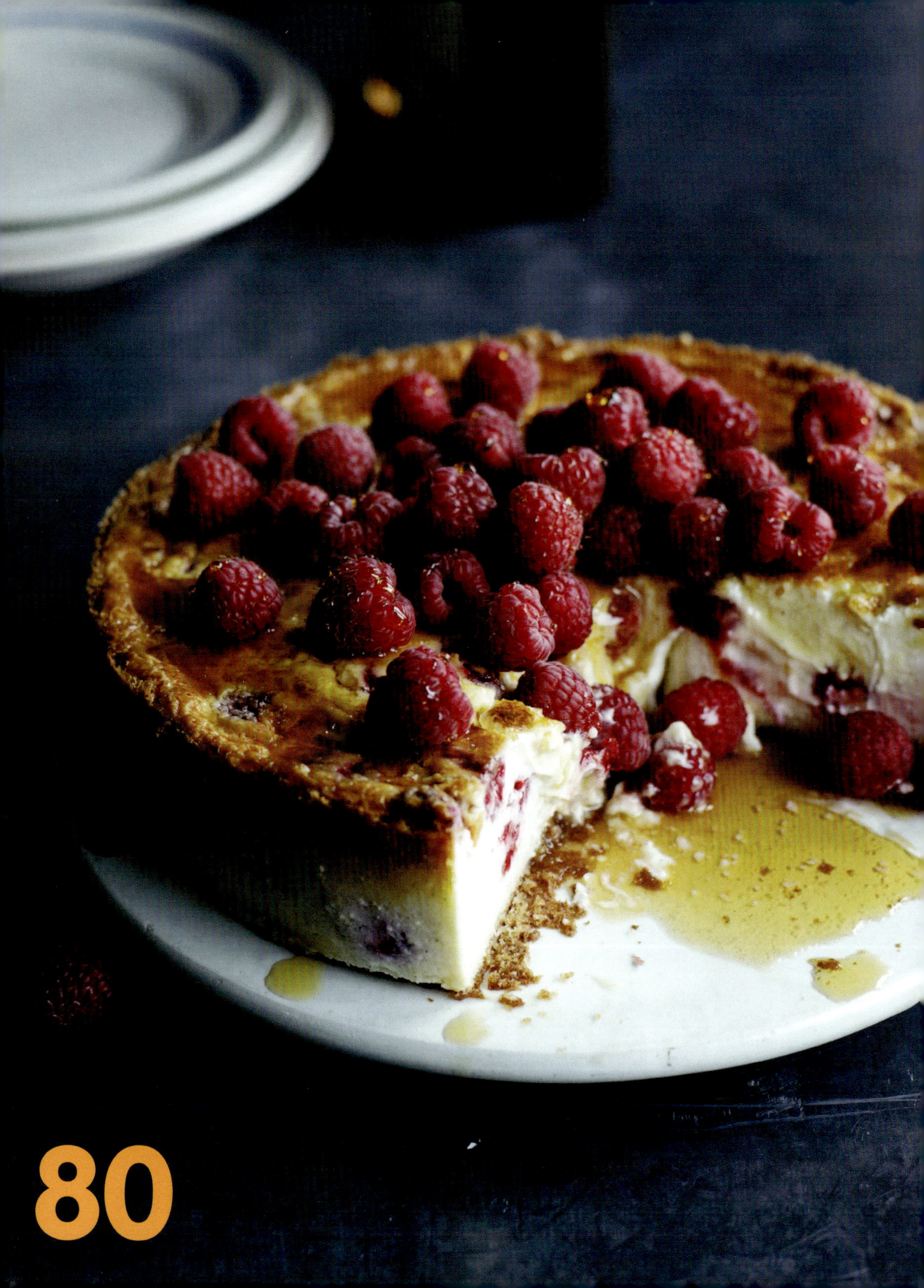

BAKED NEW YORK RASPBERRY CHEESECAKE
from James Martin
Serves 6-8

Ingredients
- 23cm sponge base
- 1 vanilla pod
- Grated zest and juice of 1 lemon
- 200g caster sugar
- 50g corn flour
- 850g full-fat soft cream cheese
- 4 large eggs
- 375ml double cream
- 400g raspberries
- 150ml maple syrup

Method
- Preheat the oven to 180°C. Slice the sponge base in half horizontally to form a 5mm thick disc, and place it in the bottom of a springform 23cm cake tin.
- Split the vanilla pod in half lengthways and scrape out the seeds. Put the vanilla seeds, lemon zest and juice, sugar, corn flour and cream cheese into a bowl and whisk together. Add the eggs, one at a time, beating well between each one. Add the double cream, whisking until the mixture is smooth, then add 250g of the raspberries and stir carefully through the mixture.
- Pour into the cake tin and tap it lightly to settle the mix. Put the cake tin into a roasting tray, then pour hot water into the tray to a depth of 2cm to create a bain marie. Bake for 1¼-1½ hours, until the top is golden and the cheesecake just set.
- Remove from the oven and allow to cool in the tin. Remove and place on a serving plate, then top with the remaining raspberries and drizzle over the maple syrup. Serve with a drizzle of double cream.

82

HEAVEN WAFFLES
BACON WAFFLES WITH CRISPY BACON, POACHED EGGS AND HOLLANDAISE SAUCE

from Kimberley Walsh
Serves 4

Ingredients
For the waffles
- 250g plain flour
- 1 tsp baking powder
- 1 tsp salt
- 1 tbsp caster sugar
- 3 medium free range eggs
- 425ml whole milk
- 115g unsalted butter, melted
- 8 slices of cooked American bacon

For the hollandaise
- 1 shallot, finely diced
- 3 peppercorns
- 1 bay leaf
- 2 tbsp white wine vinegar
- 2 tbsp water
- 125g butter, melted
- 1 lemon, juiced
- 2 tsp white wine vinegar
- 2 large free range egg yolks

For the eggs and bacon
- 2 tbsp white wine vinegar
- 4 medium free range eggs
- 12 slices streaky bacon
- 2-3 tbsp fresh chives, finely chopped

Method
For the waffles
- Preheat a waffle maker to a medium setting. Preheat the oven to 140°C.
- Mix the flour, baking powder, salt and sugar in a large mixing bowl. Whisk in the eggs, milk and butter until well combined.
- Ladle some of the batter into each well of the waffle maker, close the lid and cook for five minutes or until golden-brown and crisp. Repeat the process until the batter is used up, keeping the cooked waffles warm on the wire rack in the oven.

For the hollandaise
- Place the shallot, bay leaf, white wine vinegar and water in a pan and reduce by half. Sieve and add to a large glass bowl.
- Place the egg yolks into the bowl with a pinch of salt. In a steady stream, slowly add the melted butter until it is all incorporated. Season with sea salt and freshly ground black pepper.

For the eggs and bacon
- Bring a pan of salted water to the boil and add the vinegar. Whisk the water to create a whirlpool and once settled, carefully crack an egg into the water. Simmer for 2-3 minutes, remove the poached egg with a slotted spoon and place onto a plate to drain. Repeat the process with the remaining eggs.
- Heat a frying pan until hot, add the bacon and cook until crisp on both sides. Drain the bacon on kitchen paper.
- To serve, place the waffles onto the serving plates, top with the poached eggs and bacon and finish with a drizzle of hollandaise sauce and the chopped chives.

"THIS IS A DELICIOUS, GREEN, SAVOURY CAKE, PACKED FULL OF SPINACH AND EGGS – VERY HEALTHY AND VERY CLEAN. OF COURSE, IF YOU WANT, YOU COULD RUIN ALL THAT BY SERVING IT WITH A PILE OF CRISPY BACON."

Bill Granger
LEEK AND SPINACH CAKE

85

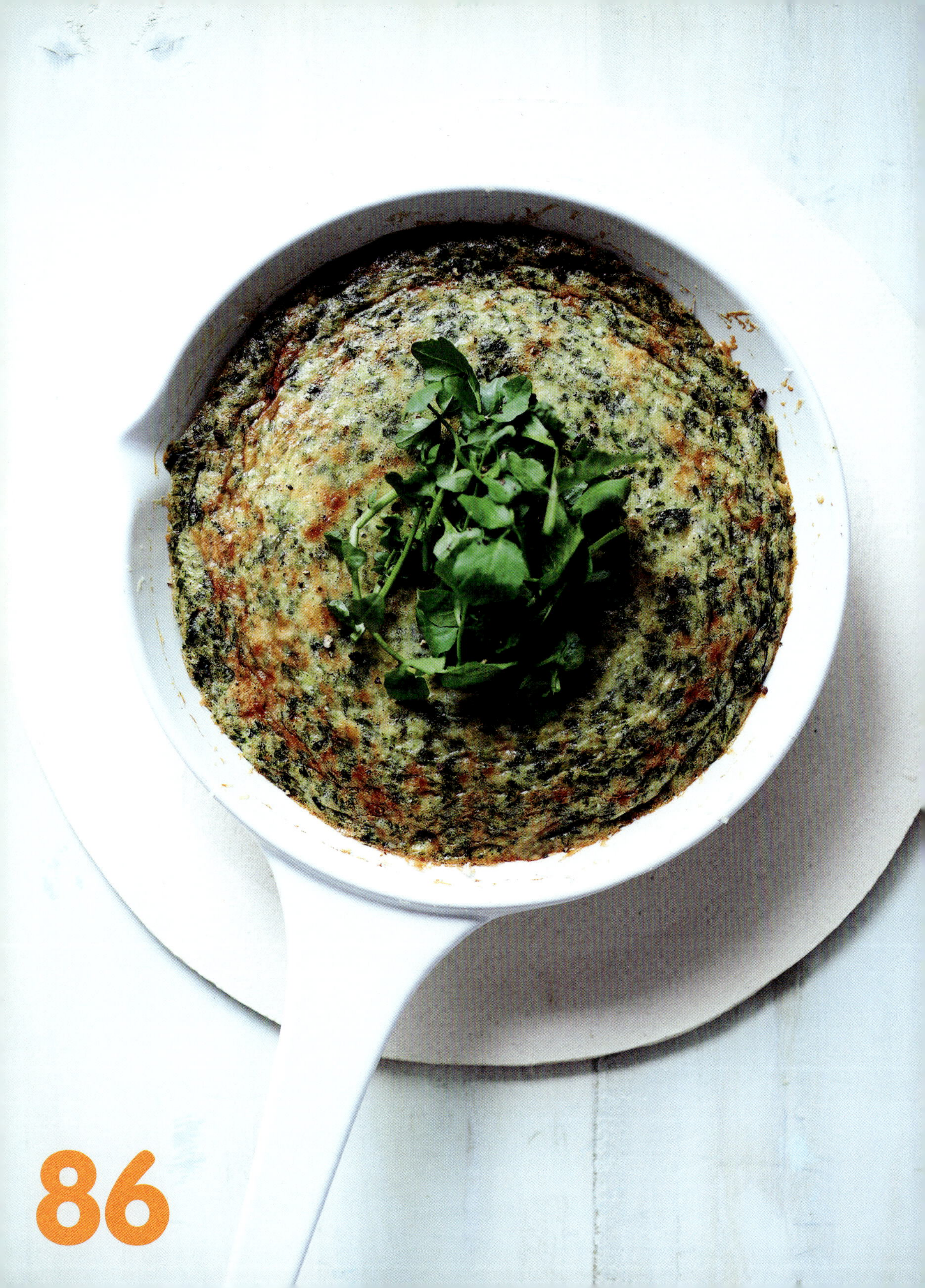

LEEK AND SPINACH CAKE
from Bill Granger
Serves 4

Ingredients
- 1 tbsp olive oil
- 15g unsalted butter
- 2 leeks, chopped
- 200g baby spinach leaves or watercress, stems removed
- 1 pinch grated nutmeg
- 125ml milk
- 6 large eggs, lightly beaten
- 25g freshly grated parmesan cheese
- Handful of watercress, to serve

Method
- Preheat the oven to 180°C and grease a medium (about 800ml) round ovenproof dish.
- Heat the oil and butter in a saucepan over medium heat. Add the leek and cook gently for about 10 minutes, until soft. Add the spinach and nutmeg and season with sea salt and freshly ground black pepper. Cover and leave to wilt for 5 minutes. Remove the spinach, increase the heat and reduce the liquid in the pan to about 1 tbsp.
- Transfer the spinach and liquid to a food processor. Add the milk and beaten egg and blend until smooth but still slightly textured. Pour into the prepared ovenproof dish and scatter with the parmesan. Bake for 25-30 minutes, until golden brown.
- Serve topped with watercress.

Recipe from **Easy** by Bill Granger (Harper Collins).

"I AM DELIGHTED TO BE AN AMBASSADOR FOR RAYS OF SUNSHINE. SPENDING TIME WITH WISH CHILDREN AND THEIR FAMILIES HAS GIVEN ME FIRSTHAND EXPERIENCE OF THE DIFFERENCE A WISH CAN MAKE AND I ENJOY HELPING OUT WHENEVER I CAN."

Lorraine Pascale

89

Lorraine's latest book, **Fast, Fresh and Easy Food** is available now, £20 by HarperCollins.

90

AUSSIE SWEETCORN BREAKFAST FRITTERS WITH AVOCADO AND ROCKET SALAD AND SWEET CHILLI JAM

from Lorraine Pascale
Serves 2

Ingredients

For the chilli jam
- 375g jar of mild or hot Peppadew peppers
- 125g cherry tomatoes
- ½ bag of fresh basil
- 6 tbsp caster sugar

For the fritters
- Sunflower oil
- 50g self-raising flour
- 50ml whole milk
- 1 egg
- 425g tin of sweetcorn
- 50g half- or full-fat crème fraîche, to serve

For the avocado & rocket salad
- 1 ripe avocado
- ½ bag of rocket
- Drizzle of extra virgin olive oil
- Drizzle of balsamic vinegar
- Salt and freshly ground black pepper

Method

- First, prepare the chilli jam. Drain the Peppadew peppers well and put them in a blender or food processor with the cherry tomatoes. Add the leaves from the basil stalks and blitz until smooth. Then tip into a medium pan over a medium heat. Add the caster sugar and bring to the boil.
- Meanwhile, start on the fritters. Put a big drizzle of oil into a large frying pan over a medium to high heat. Put the flour, milk and egg in a medium bowl or jug with a big pinch of salt and some pepper. Beat the mixture hard with a wooden spoon to get rid of any lumps. Drain the sweetcorn well, stir into the batter and set aside for a moment.
- Once the chilli jam is boiling, turn down the heat and leave it to simmer away for 8 minutes, stirring it from time to time so that it does not catch on the bottom.
- Once the oil in the frying pan is nice and hot, put four dollops of the fritter mix into the pan. Each one should be about 10cm in diameter and this uses all of the mixture up. Cook for about 3 minutes.
- Meanwhile, cut the avocado in half and remove the stone. The easiest way to get the stone out is to put the blade of a sharp knife into the stone as if you were going to cut it in half. Then twist the knife a bit and the stone should just pop out. Peel off the skin and slice the flesh into long, thin strips. Arrange to one side of two serving plates and set aside for a moment.
- The underside of the fritters should now be crisp and golden brown, so flip them over and leave to cook for another 3 minutes.
- Pile the rocket into the centre of each plate, drizzle with a little oil and balsamic vinegar. Once the fritters are crisp and golden on the bottom, remove them from the heat and arrange two of them on each plate opposite the avocado. Dollop the crème fraîche beside them. Remove the now-reduced chilli jam from the heat and spoon a little onto each plate. Give a little twist of black pepper over everything and serve.
- Any remaining chilli jam can be stored in a sterilised jar in the fridge for up to one month. It is also delicious served with meats and cheeses.

TOFU SCRAMBLE
from Leona Lewis
Serves 2

Ingredients
- 400g block extra-firm tofu
- 2 tbsp sunflower oil
- 1 small onion, chopped
- ¼ bag of spinach, washed thoroughly and dried
- 2 large tomatoes, chopped
- 1 avocado diced
- 2 vegetarian sausages

Method
- Place tofu on a plate lined with several layers of paper towels (to absorb liquid). Use a fork or potato masher to mash the tofu.
- Heat oil in a large frying pan over medium heat and cook the onions until softened.
- Add the spinach, cook for a few moments then drain the liquid. Add the chopped tomatoes.
- Grill the sausages first then slice and add to the pan.
- Stir in the tofu and cook through. Season with salt and pepper.
- Serve with the diced avocado.

93

"A FULL ENGLISH BREAKFAST IS AN INSTITUTION AND ONE OF THE BEST-KNOWN NATIONAL MEALS IN THE WORLD. FOR LARGER NUMBERS IT CAN BE TRICKY TO GET ALL THE COMPONENTS READY AT THE SAME TIME. A QUICK AND EASY SOLUTION IS AN ALL-IN-ONE FRITTATA. TO PREPARE THIS AHEAD (NO MORE THAN 2 HOURS IN ADVANCE), COMPLETE ALL THE STEPS BEFORE ADDING THE EGGS. THEN, WHEN YOU ARE READY TO SERVE, SIMPLY REHEAT THE BASE INGREDIENTS, ADD THE BEATEN EGGS AND POP IT UNDER THE GRILL."

—FULL ENGLISH FRITTATA
from Pippa Middleton
Serves 8 (makes 2 frittatas)

—Ingredients
- 4 tbsp olive oil
- 6 sausages, cut into chunks
- 12 slices streaky bacon, cut into bite-size pieces
- 400g baby portobello or small flat mushrooms, halved
- 16 cherry tomatoes, halved
- 16 free-range eggs
- Salt and freshly ground black pepper
- 150g cheddar cheese, grated

—Method
- Preheat the grill to high.
- Divide the oil between two 26cm oven-proof frying pans and heat, then divide the sausages between the pans.
- Sauté for a few minutes to colour them before adding half the bacon to each pan.
- Continue to cook for a further 2-3 minutes. Add the mushrooms to each pan, and fry for 5-6 minutes.
- Divide the cherry tomatoes between the pans and cook for a further minute.
- In a bowl, whisk the eggs and season generously. Pour half the egg mixture into each pan and cook over a gentle heat for 8-10 minutes to set the base. Scatter half the cheese over one frittata, then transfer the pan to the grill and cook for 4-5 minutes or until lightly golden and set. Do the same with the remaining cheese and the second frittata. When the frittatas have cooled slightly, cut each into wedges to serve.

Recipe from **Celebrate** by Pippa Middleton, £25 Hardback (Penguin Books)

"I FIRST BECAME AWARE OF THE CHARITY THROUGH MEETING THEIR SPECIAL AMBASSADOR, FORMER WISH CHILD ALICE HALSTEAD, AN AMAZING YOUNG WOMAN WHOSE LIFE HAS UNDOUBTEDLY BEEN TOUCHED BY THE POWER OF A RAYS OF SUNSHINE WISH. I AM HONOURED TO BE AN AMBASSADOR AND HOPE I CAN HELP THE CHARITY TO BRIGHTEN UP THE LIVES OF EVEN MORE DESERVING CHILDREN AND YOUNG PEOPLE."

Amanda Lamb

97

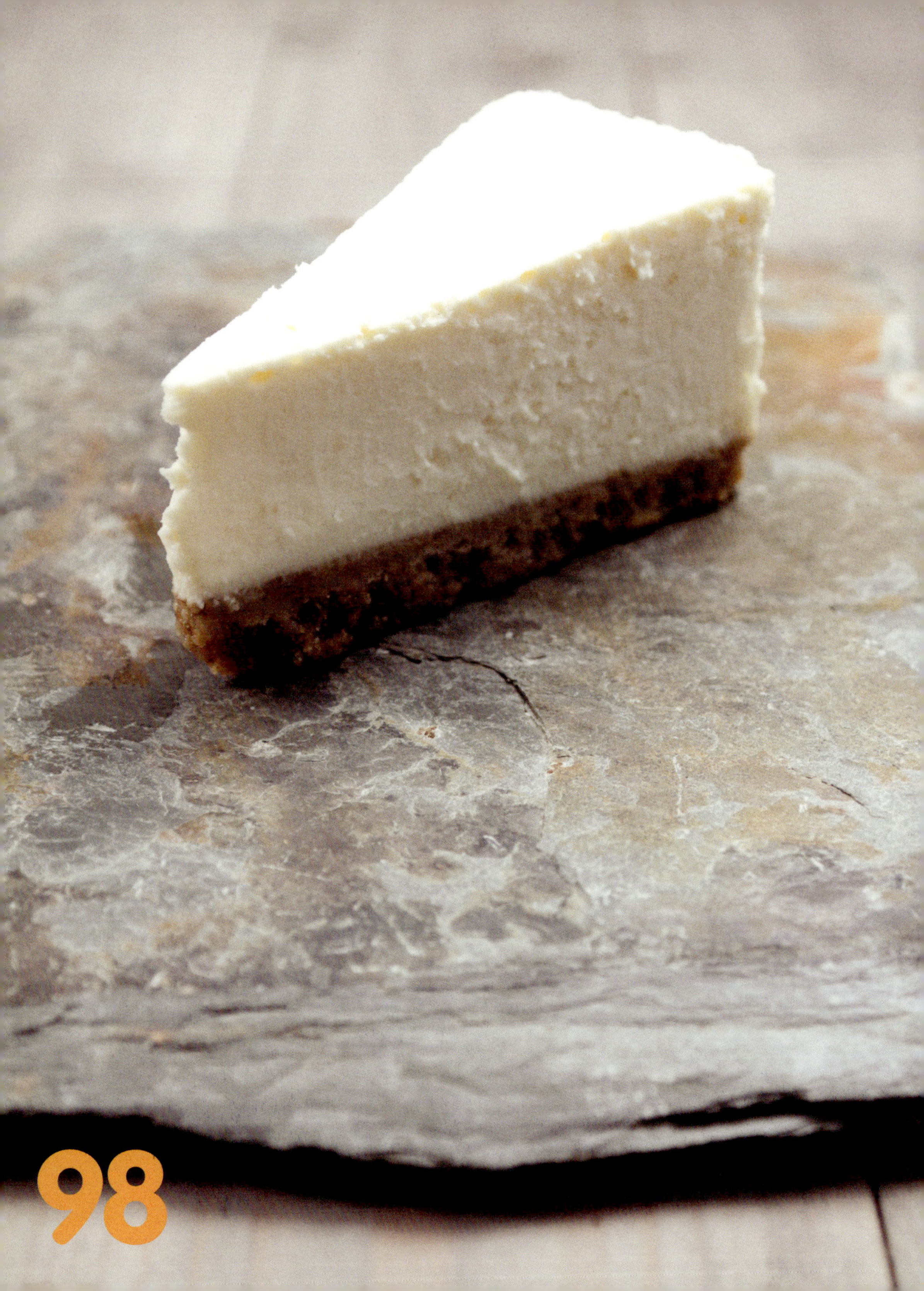

VANILLA CHEESECAKE
from Amanda Lamb
Serves 6

Ingredients
- 200g digestive biscuits
- 50g butter, diced
- 740g full-fat cream cheese, such as Philadelphia
- 225g golden caster sugar
- 3 tbsp cornflour
- 2 vanilla pods, seeds only
- Few drops vanilla extract
- 2 eggs, beaten
- 240ml double cream

Method
- Preheat the oven to 180°C. Grease a 20-24cm round, springform cake tin. Break the biscuits into a blender and process to a crumbs. Melt the butter in a small pan and mix with the biscuit crumbs.
- Tip the mixture into the cake tin and press firmly over the base to make an even 1cm thick layer. Chill for about 30 minutes.
- Using an electric mixer on its slowest setting, combine the cheese, sugar, cornflour, vanilla seeds and extract until smooth and thick. Add the eggs and cream and continue to mix until very thick.
- Spoon into the tin and smooth the top. Bake for 45 minutes or until set in the centre, then increase the oven temperature to 200°C for 10 minutes to brown the top. Remove from the oven and leave until cold, then chill in the fridge until ready to serve.

"WE ARE SO GRATEFUL TO OUR FAMOUS SUPPORTERS FOR GIVING UP THEIR TIME TO HELP MAKE WISHES COME TRUE AND FOR SHARING THEIR FAVOURITE BREAKFAST AND BRUNCH RECIPES WITH US. WE HOPE THAT THIS BOOK WILL HELP TURN EVERY BREAKFAST INTO A SPECIAL OCCASION."

Jane Sharpe
Chief Executive
Rays of Sunshine Children's Charity

THANK
YOU

101

Zane and Niamh

Megan and Oritsé

Murad and Aston

Olly and Amber-Leigh

Elijah and Fireman Sam

Debra Meaden, Charlie and Theo Paphitis

JLS with Georgia

Wasim & Gordon Ramsay

Joss and Dynamo the Magician

Faith and Lorraine Pascale

Louis and Niamh

Liam with Meghan

Rachel and Nathan with Lorraine Pascale

Celebrating our 10th birthday with Chancellor George Osborne at Downing Street

Amber and Aston

Charlie and Louis Smith

102

Marvin and Milly

Milly and Iona

Jack and Olly Murs

Cassie with One Direction

Oscar at Disneyland, Paris

Union J with Jessica

Hannah, Lisa Snowdon and Ellie-Mai

Danny Welbeck, Noah, Anthony and Phil Jones

Kimberley with Jessica

Ruby

Richard Hammond and Emilia

Shannon & Conor Maynard

Niall and Grace

103

Niamh with One Direction

Olly Murs with Samuel

Joe Hart with Jacob

Our outing to Legoland

Ray and Sunshine at The Rays of Sunshine Concert

The Luminites at The Rays of Sunshine Teenage Party

Lauren and Linden the Mermaid

Enna at Lapland

Dynamo the Magician and Jack

Pixie and Louis at The Teenage Party

Kiera and The Wanted

Ellie and Harry Styles

Miley and Bel

Amber being a model for the day

Charlotte being a paramedic for the day

104